Dining with
John the Baptist

Dining with John the Baptist

POEMS

Thomas Ronald Vaughan

RESOURCE *Publications* • Eugene, Oregon

DINING WITH JOHN THE BAPTIST
Poems

Copyright © 2021 Thomas Ronald Vaughan. All rights reserved. Except for brief quotations in critical publications or reviews, no part of this book may be reproduced in any manner without prior written permission from the publisher. Write: Permissions, Wipf and Stock Publishers, 199 W. 8th Ave., Suite 3, Eugene, OR 97401.

Resource Publications
An Imprint of Wipf and Stock Publishers
199 W. 8th Ave., Suite 3
Eugene, OR 97401

www.wipfandstock.com

PAPERBACK ISBN: 978-1-7252-9775-3
HARDCOVER ISBN: 978-1-7252-9776-0
EBOOK ISBN: 978-1-7252-9777-7

03/31/21

Many of these poems were written during lockdown times caused by the COVID-19 pandemic. I was reminded again that the Greek word *therapeia*—our "therapy"—includes the reading and writing of poetry. I hope that some verses here will be of benefit, during this unusual time, to my solitary reader.

A NEW PSALM

Tears well in my eyes as he takes the stage,
And led by the father's hand
He loudly sings, "Open the eyes of my heart, Lord,
Open the eyes of my heart. . . . ."
There are things to say here.
One, he is merely a "Polly Wants A Cracker " parrot.
Two, the very Lord God Almighty indwells his every tentative syllable.
I choose the latter,
So God cannot mind if I paraphrase the verse,
"Out of the mouths of babes and
Ten-year old blind, autistic children,
Hast thou ordained strength."
Sing, child, sing!
Then take my trembling hand and join me
Beside this tough and terrible road.
Surely, soon, it must be that
The King is coming.
He will know you when he hears you.

Matthew 20: 30: As Jesus passed by, the blind men cried out.

SCHOPENHAUER MAKES HIS CASE

If you lead the most unrepentant optimists
Through all the dark dwellings of misery
That hide from cold curiosity,
They will most certainly fly into a kind of Stoicism.
"Right thinking" is what saves,
Ataraxia, the only hope.
      Every day he played the flute,
Ate a delicious meal,
Smoked a cigar,
Walked the pet dog.
Without God, what else is there?

Arthur Schopenhauer (1788–1860), German philosopher, wrote *The World as Will and Representation*

EASTER POEM

Christ, I crave your peace.
In this chair of my disjunct existence
I seek a wholeness,
Your wholeness.
Pledge me a point at which
All my divergent passions unite:
It will be in you.
Draw me forward to that mark,
Extracting from me what displeases you most.
Push me toward that elemental education
Producing within, forever,
What you will have me become.
I crave your peace.
O Christ, I seek your wholeness.
Send the purifying fire!
May my residue hear you say, "Blessed!"

THE FIRST SAMARITAN

Friend, I would stop and help,
But as you see my load
Is more than I can bear
On this hot, dusty road.

So wipe your bloody head,
Another will come by
Whose burden will be light —
More medical than I.

Then we can part as friends,
And I will journey on,
Assured that it was best
If you be left alone.

Good luck, and may God bless!
Beware the heat of day.
I would be sore distressed
If more ill came your way.

Samaritan story, Luke 10

DISRESPECTFULLY, FOR CHARLES DARWIN

If souls were born of water
After the world began,
I have no definition
Quite suitable for "man."

For I have seen the creatures
That come up from the sea
And I am quite discouraged
If part of them is "me."

If they are part of me,
And part of me is them,
How to explain my loathing
To ever have a swim!

Charles Darwin (1809–1882), English naturalist, wrote, *On the Origin of Species*

GIRL ON A BALCONY

We will never know
If the "girl with one leg"
Was leaning over the balcony
To see the car
Or to take her own life.
Dr. William Carlos Williams should have told us
But he did not.
Apparently, he paused to look,
And only look,
Then drove on by.

William Carlos Williams (1883–1963), American poet and physician, wrote "The Right of Way"

DIONYSUS AND ARIADNE

My love for Dithyrambic came with costs.
I think I met him once when I was young.
I fear that I recall nothing at all,
Except the slurring of his winey tongue.

Once dined with Ariadne in a maze,
A labyrinthine thing which few escape.
It was a lovely evening, nonetheless,
Just sitting on the thin Sideros Cape.

She left me here, and here I am today,
Chanting in Latin and speaking in Greek.
I flee to Mount Olympus in my mind,
Hoping the pilgrims find the life they seek.

Characters from Greek mythology

FOR PASTOR, BEFORE THE MASTECTOMY

Soon, you will lie on a cold table
Of skill and pain, disfigurement and hope.
We cannot be there, nor should we,
But we can embrace you,
Golden hair, like unharvested wheat,
Eyes and smile that invite us in,
Words that say, "It is safe here;
Our lives are much alike."
We think of the myriad times
You invited us to stand
And say what we believe.
I, poor congregant, despairing of this night,
Shout in my confession,
Of rage and helplessness,
That you, dear one,
Are yesterday, today, and forever, whole,
That your necessary sleep
Of icy, surgical precision
Will diminish you in no way at all.

THE LAST DAYS OF SIGMUND FREUD

Was something sacred in that rotting head
To spawn the dedication of a daughter,
Who served him at his final couch and bed,
Who brought the analytic bread and water?

And what engaged that aging Jewish head,
In line with dreaming prophets long since dead:
A fight with God, and did that mind rebel —-
Could only Death the "boiling cauldron" quell?

Sigmund Freud (1856–1939), father of Psychoanalysis; Anna Freud (1895–1982), Analyst, Freud's daughter

MY AGING DINOSAUR

My aging dinosaur moves with a jolt,
Craning his creaking neck, slinging his spit,
Watching the brontosaurus in the grass,
And glaring mockingly because of it.

You see it is red flesh that makes him drool,
Red meat in chunks and pounds that he ingests.
A tear, a rip, a chomp—it all goes down.
That is the menu item he requests.

I raised him from a baby in the egg.
He has delighted me since he was born.
Precocious, prodigy, and other terms
Most fittingly his pedigree adorn.

I grieve over the stiffness in his joints.
Time was his gait was crisp, his movements clean.
I give him medically the best I can—
Daily chondroitin and glucosamine.

We age together like the best of friends.
I tell him tales as we sit down and rock:
The glories of the lost Jurassic days,
And wishing we could both turn back the clock.

THE BEAUTIFUL NEVER CHANGES

Spring
Comes into
My heart
And
My heart
Turns.

I
Loved you
All my life
In blue
Lucernes.

For Richard Wilbur (1921–2017), American poet, wrote "The Beautiful Changes." Lucerne: plant with blue-green flowers, grown as a pasture

MILITARY CHAPLAIN

Many the hill we have taken,
Taken at terrible cost.
Many the battles we fought in,
Many the battles we lost.

Many the fields we abandoned,
Pointless sustaining the fight.
Leaving those fields to the rival,
Turning the colors in flight.

Many the heart I have broken,
My acting, never so brave,
Telling the spouse or the lover
Our best was not able to save.

SHACKLETON ABANDONS HIS SHIP

In its brute drudgery
Life seldom offers choice,
But when it does a man
Should in his soul rejoice.

When Shackleton threw down
Gold coins upon the ice,
He saved a book of verse,
And said, "This will suffice."

Yet in the world betimes,
Men need a little gold,
And every man can tell
If it will cost his soul.

Ernest Shackleton (1874–1922), Irish Polar explorer, lost his ship, saved the entire crew, died heavily in debt

GOING THE SAME WAY

In Tunguska, Arctic Russia, I was reminded
Of the distinct possibility of Life extinction
By a random strike from a wily asteroid.
Awed Kulik viewed the boreal wreckage
And stared in fearful wonder
At the vast and silent night.
In 20's Siberia no one
Could predict such a coming.
Our horror now would be to see it,
Knowing it was the End,
Able only to plan for the inevitability.
As the heavy brachiosaurus, chomping gingko,
Did not sense that all her marvelous species
Would soon stagger, crash to the earth,
Never to rise again.
How interesting, I ruminate,
Returning to my cold, crisp salad
And very dry white wine.

Mysterious explosion in Tunguska, Siberia, 1908, explored in 1921 by scientist Leonid Kulik

AIDS

Farewell to those who love me.
Farewell to those who don't.
Farewell to those who'll miss me.
Farewell to those who won't.

Farewell to Winter weather;
I will not see the Spring.
I spent one reckless Summer,
But still it makes me sing.

THE LAST THYLACINE

While brutish tourists tortured every move,
I saw you frantic in a too small cage.
I think you understood your sentence well.
You did not yelp; this was not badinage.

A strange carnivorous marsupial
Was not a cause to urgently insist,
And so you passed into oblivion,
Odd name upon some species obit list.

Yet, dreamers dream you are still roaming free,
A fox-faced tiger in the Tasman night,
Catching an unsuspecting wallaby,
Then vanishing at dawn's first ray of light.

Last filmed in the early 30's, declared extinct in 1936

HOPE SPRINGS ETERNAL

Hope springs eternal in the breast;
It does not spring in mine.
For I have tasted of the earth
And I have tasted brine.

For not a day goes by but that
Lost children writhe in pain,
And lovers look in lover's eyes,
And do not look again.

STREET MALLARD

I have never been this close to your beauty,
Coming out into the road to scoop you
In an old shovel,
Saving you from four crows
Loudly objecting to my action.
They need not fear
For I will throw you into the wood
And they can make their choices.
Nature must always win.
As I hold you in this rusty spade
I turn you this way and that.
In the clear morning light
Your plumage reveals
A myriad of tints and hues,
Spectacular, as they are stunning.
Now flinging you away,
I have no choice but to wonder,
In my anthropomorphic simplicity,
If you have been at all aware
Of your magnificent, flashing adornment.

NUMBERS

I counted all the numbers,
Then counted them again.
Still four and three make seven,
And five and five make ten.

Yes, three and four are seven,
And two and three are five.
But when the coin is passion,
The figures are alive!

AUTOPSY

And since I could not fathom death,
Death roughly fathomed me.
Now I must lie completely still
For gross anatomy.

They will not find the bullet.
They will not find the pill.
I died of the illusion
That it was death I'd kill.

After Emily Dickinson (1830–1886), American poet, wrote "Because I could not stop for Death"

SHE PURRS WITH CLAWS

"Can't we just be friends?"
Finally, the words have come,
Inevitable as the morning sun,
But nothing warm here.
Graham Greene said it was the End,
But she is not sick, you are sure.
These things are centripetal,
But that one sentence knocks the orbit.
Like a particle accelerator.
You spin off on your own, not looking back.
There is nothing to see now.
You cannot think of it further,
Spending absolutely no time
Defining any of the eviscerating words
In her scratching remark.
And while you believe in mutation, metamorphosis, and change,
It is highly appropriate to assume
That in none of her nine exotic lives
The words will ever be different.
Well do you remember the warm nights of sleepy purrs,
But now have come the dreaded razor claws.
There is no defense.

Graham Greene (1904-1991), English novelist, wrote *The End of the Affair*

SOME AUSTEN WOMEN

Excessive when unhappy,
Restrained when feeling well,
His money flew to vendors,
Symbolic of their Hell.

But what a large endowment,
So many pounds a year!
Important for a moment,
But what a price paid— dear.

To love or love for money?
An age of female dread,
Enslavement in the System,
And terror in the bed.

Jane Austen (1775–1817), English novelist

NAZI BOOK BURNING

It is a well-known fact that
Fire creates its own wind,
And sometimes, despite the author,
Or title, or subject,
Books thrown into flames
Attempt to escape the immolation
By opening and literally flying upward
Like a fleeing bird.
Inevitably the pages disintegrate,
Turn to ash and disappear.
But against the chants of a hostile, raging, mob
The defiance is brief, mysterious, apparitional, angelic.
Interestingly, however, ideas neither burn
Nor flutter away shimmering
Into any frightening, threatening,
Or murderous night sky.

For George Prochnik (1961—present), contemporary Jewish author

OTHER THOUGHTS TO THINK

Other thoughts to think, I thought them,
Other words to say.
Mine, the solitary sadness,
Mine, the price to pay.

Other lives to live, I lived them,
Other tales to tell.
It, the perfect part for players,
And I played It well.

Other dreams to dream, I dreamed them,
Other sights to see.
Virtuous the single eye,
And you are not with me.

TERESA'S ECSTASY

There is something maddening about it.
If you close your eyes and listen,
You can listen to the right or left.
Amazing!
There is something there,
Out there or in there,
All the time.
Only in those moments do you feel it.
Many have said, "God!"
Have said, "I have communed with God!"
There is something.
You can sense its approach,
And in that darkness it comes,
Hovering like a thick fog.
If you dare to look: nothing.
But eyes closed you are filled with "Presence."
You are terrified, afraid, trembling,
But your knees bend, your arms open,
And your desperate, yearning spirit begs,
"Ravish me! Ravish me!"

Saint Teresa of Avila (1515–1582), Spanish mystic

UNSPOKEN

Patina on my broken heart,
It shines as purest gold.
So many things I could have said,
So many things untold.

For through your vast, imploring eyes
I saw your heart grow weak.
But well defended, troubled men
May think, but seldom speak.

On winter days especially now,
I dream and walk about,
And to the frozen, senseless snow
I find my voice and shout.

ICE CREAM HEADACHE

It is a migraine pulse,
From which,
If relief did not come,
You would consider suicide.
But when the pain abates
You slow down,
Swallow,
Lick again,
And discuss
In humorous conversation.

LAZARUS

"By now he stinks,"
    Said the lady
    Using her head.
"Don't let them open that tomb!
Don't experiment with my brother, you cranks!"
    And the people stood by,
    Mostly in shock,
    Waiting for the law.
Then the mummy limped out,
Protesting and shouting,
"Why did you bring me back to die again!"
    But everyone else
    Stopped using their heads
    And were wildly happy.

Lazarus story, John 11

THE SHORE

All that is left,
As in Stevens' "Fabliau of Florida,"
Is the barque and the droning sea.
No first slime looks to land,
And no dumb, odd thing
Drools and looks
Seaward insipidly.

All that is left is the barque
And the listless sea,
Forever taking those little laps and licks
Which pop and crackle
And irritate to a fit of rage,
When the sea was supposed
To bring solace.

Wallace Stevens (1879–1955), American poet, wrote of the droning sea: ". . . there will never be an end."

CHEYNE-STOKES

The chest heaves up and then it does not heave.
The daughter drops her hand and gasps for air.
A nurse applies the gentle stethoscope,
Then shakes her head inviting this despair.

The nodding priest awakes and stumbles up
Reciting words that he does not believe.
He has been more than faithful through it all,
And stayed the night though often urged to leave.

She was a famous singer from the East,
Her operatic voice enchanting, clear.
Cheyne-Stokes came by to join her yesterday:
Strange coda of a brilliant career.

Cheyne-Stokes, the so-called end of life "death rattle"

THE END OF ADOLESCENCE

As a high school student in Norfolk, Virginia,
I developed the unique skill
Of forging teachers' signatures
So that I and my unlawful friends
Could skip classes.
Inevitably, someone was caught red handed,
But fortunately did not rat me out.
Unrepentant and defiant, I clandestinely
Continued my sinister, nefarious ways.
Eventually the year ended,
And regretfully I relocated to Northwest Florida.
There, I discovered to my chagrin that no one needed
My no-fee, exquisite services.
(Though I did once carry Moonshine in my too- cool car.)
The following Fall I was far away, ensconced in college,
Oddly preparing for Christian ministry.
I can declare in sincere confession
That this most unlikely decision was not at all
Reactive to my sordid, wasteful, wastrel life of crime.
There were other reasons entirely.

THE DEATH OF ELVIS PRESLEY

I was suddenly older,
Having lost you a friend from childhood.
I would say
That mostly we sang together.
You did all of the things I dreamed of
Part of the time.
I would want you to know,
Above all,
That I never took offense
Even when we grew up
And went our very separate ways.

Elvis Presley (1935–1977), American entertainment icon

QUITE SLOW

Quite slow to come around,
I hold you in my arms
And find that I am bound
By much more than your charms.

Though charms are very nice,
And chemistry desire,
And we would not look twice
Unless we felt that fire.

I will not let you go
When passion fades away,
For Ordinary calls,
And Life lives day by day.

CARRIER PILOT, MIDWAY

That boy just shot a Zero from the sky,
And sent another off, trailing in smoke.
We call him, "Emily" because he came
From Massachusetts, near Mt. Holyoke.

We should not be familiar with this youth.
In fact, we should not even learn his name.
It's best, for when he sputters in to land,
He clips a wing and flips, bursting in flame.

Battle of Midway, World War II, 1942. Planes lost USA, 145; Japan, 292

THE IMAGISTS

Sarah Teasdale on a cow,
William Carlos on a bull,
Imaging their way along,
Pages after pages full.

Operations all complete,
Men can strum their blue guitars,
While the lighter on their feet
Scan the heavens for bright stars.

Imagism, 20th Century poetry movement

FAMILY PLOT

He finished what they started;
He sent them all to "school."
He taught them to "love Jesus,"
And keep The Golden Rule.

I visit on some Sundays.
I keep the vases clean.
The children lie beside them,
Quite lovely, quite serene.

Always, the night sky darkens,
And blooming flowers decay.
The seasons turn in sequence,
And nothing here can stay.

COLD MORNINGS

Cold mornings in December,
I dream of early Spring,
To see some flowers blooming,
Hear just one robin sing.

And I have noticed often,
When doom is in the air,
That I am aided mostly
By things that are not there.

SIRENS

"A stitch in time saves nine," they say.
Who said it, said it right.
Then what I squandered yesterday
I may regain by night.

But now the tempting Sirens sing,
"Come, come! You must not wait!"
So I rewrite the line to read,
"The stitch saves only eight."

Temptress voices, from Greek mythology

PHYSICALLY, THE BODY OF ABISHAG

I sour of my wives and concubines.
This chill I feel is not because I'm old.
Attending me are incompetent fools.
I laugh because they think that I am cold!

They bring me much more beauty than they ought,
Suspecting she is here to save my life.
Disrobing, she reminds me of my youth,
And of my first encounter with a wife.

Young women flash into my pulsing mind,
Those women that I loved and who loved me.
Lay down, my pretty one, and take my hand.
No one will write of what they cannot see.

Story of David and Abishag, I Kings 1

SUICIDE FUNERAL

I do not feel guilty for "missing" this,
Since everyone known to you did.
There is a mysterious Psychiatrist somewhere,
But I remember working in a State Hospital,
And after casual, pleasant conversations,
Hearing that the attempt failed,
And all was well.
There is "Gospel" here, and I search for it,
Trying to separate your deed from
Our theological magisterium.
I can do it, for I have done it before,
Remembering that today I must not mention
The smoking shotgun, the incompletion, the rage,
And, mostly, the lack of sensible answers.
Only hope and grace.
I have loved you, and will sorely miss you,
Even as I could rush to your casket,
Shake you angrily, and give you
A tear-filled and final embrace.
But I will not do that.
Collecting myself professionally,
I stare at the stunned congregation,
"The Lord be with you. . . . ."

SUPERFLUOUS DAUGHTERS

Since none came forward from the countryside,
No prince, no silly farmer in the dale,
They gave the dowry to the nunnery,
Insisting that these daughters take the veil.

And so their lot was cast into a life
Of wimples and soft bells jingling for prayer,
And endless fingering the rosary,
And staring dismally through smoky air.

Even the Holy Supper could not save.
The coughing priest was never heard by God.
And for the years of that redundancy
Sweet nuns embrace the hungry roots and sod.

For Eileen Power (1889–1940), English historian, wrote *Medieval English Nunneries*

HOMAGE TO LOUISIANA

A hungry dog makes music in the swamp.
The snappers and the alligators croon.
I cannot find a reason for this noise,
Except the rising of the dusky moon.

I love these Bayou evenings on a porch,
With jambalaya wafting through the air;
A Cajun band beginning to explode
To make us think Evangeline is near.

Assertive in the Gulf of Mexico,
Its ancient Delta seems forever new.
The River gifting islands with its silt:
This Louisiana is a point of view!

THAT TIME

That time he came for victory,
In finest armor clad.
He'd hoped to leave with her consent,
Immeasurably glad.

But how could youth so wrongly read,
Or so misprise a heart,
That worlds he hoped they would construct
Would shake and fall apart.

MIDNIGHT IN THE MIDDLE PASSAGE

Yes, there is stench and oozing and excrement.
Do not jump.
Or go ahead tomorrow.
The water is indifferent,
And they lose only money.
Sit up and think.
You cannot sit up.
These rows and rows are flat.
Only eighteen-inch men can stand here.
What is my skill, my trade, my blood?
Here I am a specimen: my teeth, my age, my muscle tone.
Can I breed? Have I two eyes?
Do not scream.
Or go ahead.
We will form a woeful chorus.
Whips will crack and cursing descend
To take part in our music.
I was not married; this man was.
Not from my village.
I never saw him before they crammed him here.
Now dead.
Yes, I ache. Yes, I can try to join in
But do not know the language.
What does our singing mean, "Amazing Grace"?

After Robert Hayden (1913–1980), American poet, wrote "The Middle Passage"

IRENE TRIPLETT

According to the news,
Irene Triplett received the last pension check
From her father's service in the Civil War.
She has also died.
Dad fought on both sides in the conflict,
But there is no indication that Irene was conflicted,
And $73.13 a month, for a very long time,
Makes all the difference in the world.
He had married a woman
Fifty years his junior,
But, hey, more common than you think
Way back then.
In the picture I saw of Irene
It did not seem to be a big deal.

True story. Ms. Triplett received her last check July, 2020; died May 31, 2020

THE ROAD

It was a Winter time, and I was lost.
The sinews of my life had ripped apart.
I analyzed sad options one by one,
And then I saw a road I knew by heart.

VAN GOGH

The room was full of color,
Palettes of every hue,
To give a world your vision,
As each one spoke to you.

The fields were rippling waters,
Which ancient workers till.
At night the stars were moving,
You could not make them still.

Eternal flowers blowing,
The trembling gifts you gave.
We stand in awe-struck wonder,
And place them on your grave.

Vincent van Gogh (1853–1890), Dutch painter

CAPTAIN BLIGH

"Goodbye! Good luck!," they chanted,
As I set off to sea.
I smiled and then saluted.
They could not follow me.

I went alone that season.
They understood the wait.
But in the South Pacific
I ran afoul of fate.

"Goodbye you fiend!," they shouted,
And pushed me out to sea.
Again I stood saluting
The H. M. S. Bounty.

Then came the proud inquiry
Where judges heard, then took
My word on every subject,
And then they closed the book.

But down in South Pacific,
Weak Christian and his clan
Never again saw England,
And died on bleak Pitcairn.

I ask, who was the traitor
Set in a briny sea?

My life has drawn the moral:
Justice or mutiny!

A man once more in honor,
A name the nation needs!
For all must come to harbor
The cargo of their deeds.

William Bligh, Captain of the Bounty, set adrift by mutineers, 1789, survived a 4000 mile journey to safety

PASTORAL COUNSELING

We talk of a father, drunk, with guns to kill,
Repeatedly beating a mother
We talked of, too.
I am impressed by his openness,
At this young man's ability
To share, so matter of factly,
This recurring scene,
As if I were taking notes for a headline.
We have just begun,
And it is I, skilless I,
Who must help him recover
The feelings that go with the crushing facts.
We will hit raw nerves,
And, if I am right,
We will laugh, cry, become afraid,
And threaten to kill,
Like the father,
Like the mother,
Like the child,
Who struggled to separate the fighters,
Who begged for them to stop.

DINING WITH JOHN THE BAPTIST

I see that oddness has its rich rewards,
Except for those demanded of their skins!
The locusts dipped in honey are a treat—
Your Kingdom preaching does pay dividends.

This barrenness has such appealing charm.
The brook that babbles can relax the soul,
Which I can most sincerely recommend.
You work as if you never will grow old.

I would prefer a peppery Shiraz.
But you have chosen not to touch red meat,
So pardon me for mentioning the wine:
It might enhance these items that we eat.

The one you follow with such ardent zeal,
And about whom you make outlandish claims,
However did you come to hold such views?
He is a Nazarene, by any name.

I have concerns about the words you say.
Why worry about Herod and his wife?
Your Gospel focuses on other things.
What do you care how prurient his life?

The evening—an unparalleled delight!
I must away to finish things begun.
But look—rough Roman soldiers trampling near.
Their angry spears are glinting in the sun.

John the Baptist stories, all four Gospels

ON HEARING OF A PREGNANCY

Months before this conception
I have seen you as "mother."
Know in your heart
That I thrill with you,
As love accumulates
For what is to come.
Then, I pray, it will burst out in joy,
And you will know a dimension
You can only learn by living.
Your young life will change,
And you become even more beautiful
In this newness that you find!
Share her with me.......

ON A PICTURE FOUND ON AN S. S. GUARD

The long, mysterious line moves to the pit.
It stretches, dizzily, back to drab vans.
Haggard, emaciated faces glide
To the edge of their final stop.
The soldiers count off:
"... 23.. . .. 24. . . .25. Halt!"
All turn right, face rugged pines,
And stare into the ditch
Of arms, legs, rags, lime, blood.
The seven millimeter rifles aim,
And at "Fire!," the limp frames buckle.
Every time it is the same.
WHY DO THEY NOT TURN AND FIGHT?
I do not understand!
Of emotion and struggle as human force,
At this place, today, I little learn.
I am educated only in military rigor,
Ballistics, and The Principle of Archimedes.
After this heartbreaking scene, they will do better.
There will appear machines of war,
Eternal flames, a new State.
But, in confused assessment, I hear ringing in my ears
Strains of things
"Blessed who go before the slaughterer dumb."
It is a long tradition, one point of view.

Cf. Isaiah 53:7. Actual photograph from German soldier

THE TIME

It was an interesting time
For those who saw it through.
The water was as white as snow,
Your eyes a China blue.

I have not felt such loneliness,
So many standing near,
Relating to no one at all,
Hiding colossal fear.

No, I will never venture back,
Never go there again.
I have the water and your eyes
Forever locked within.

THE UNIVERSALISTS IN NORTH CAROLINA

Down in eastern North Carolina
There are a couple of Universalist Churches
Started in the 1800's.
And you can imagine them coming into this state
Telling of all sinners being saved,
Snatched out of the fire
By a God of love.
Well, you know what a tough time they had of it,
And it is quite remarkable they exist at all today,
But a couple of Churches do, over in eastern North Carolina.
Which I wrote the Society asking for information,
And this little old lady (I can see her now)
Wrote me back saying their purpose
Was to promote the cause of Universalism in North Carolina.
I was so glad to get that letter
Because it is good to know, since not many things
Stick to the reason for which they were started.
But not the Universalists around here,
According to the letter I got
From the little old lady who is
I guess,
The Secretary of the Universalist Society of eastern North Carolina,
Still going strong.

DYLAN THOMAS

You, Dylan Thomas, from the dark hill of Wales,
As Druid, not Druid, prophet, priest, solitary wanderer,
Caught up in a breathing wind's fire,
Wrote and cursed and touched a many a fearful heart.
You, as a wise man, were wise enough to see
That men have meanings which words do not.
You, in a child's world globe,
Charged and raged and laughed with the laughing,
And acting said you would act no more.
Where, Dylan Thomas, do you behind your scribbled ink lie dead?
All cannot be jest from a man
Whose contradictions were so defenseless, so human.
      In your thirty-ninth year to heaven,
Your pen dropped, your cursing ceased,
Your insane habits took their toll.
I could, I could weep a long night's tears for you, Dylan Thomas.
Feeling your lines through my heart's impulsive hands,
I have touched your fleshy life here and there and again.
Gone, but not gone, I see you, Dylan Thomas,
Sitting in your glory on the Sun's right hand,
And with every lipped phrase I hear, not words,
But your passionate intensity.
You, Dylan Thomas, in your half-drunken dream,
Did spit and splay in the weak world's eye
A watery vision of the pregnant word's power!

Dylan Thomas (1914–1953), Welsh poet

IMPORTUNITY

I called, you did not answer.
I called, you were away.
I thought I heard one whisper,
"Come back another day.
Come back one early morning,
And wait, and if you will,
You shall be given wisdom
To aid your waiting still."

NEANDERTHALS

In the beginning these strange hominids walked.
Their sense of existence, self-preservation,
Avoidance of pain, seeking of pleasure.
They roamed the land, trapped, killed,
Thrust long spears with deadly success.
They had companions of the cave,
A community of primitives,
Crude, superstitious, and afraid.
By day they fought the world for food.
By night they kept the vigil
Of the warm and guttering fire.

THE ROOM OF BELLS

There is no need to think;
It will do you no good.
The bells forever ring
And do just what they should.

There is no exit here,
Much better men have said,
Not from the Room of Bells,
Which ring inside your head.

EX OPERE OPERATO

The cloud of perfume filled my head.
Through puzzled windows
I looked for a dignity-straightening sign.
In my arms I held the world's sleepy future,
But as wet fingers moved to her head,
No Christian was born,
No sin crushed,
No future secured,
No metaphysic moved aside.
Nothing happened.
No one could tell me what was done,
And I was, frankly,
A bit embarrassed by it all.
I have lost my faith.

Ex opere operato: a Sacrament is the action of God, and its efficacy not dependent on either Priest or recipient

A SHOPPER'S GUIDE TO PRAYER

Historically speaking, your best bet is to pray
That God's will coincides with yours.
That way, you can become the center of attention
In circles which actually speak of such things.
Alternatively, there is the selfish prayer,
Especially useful when you're down and out.
A lot of folks get a lot of mileage
By using, "I," "my," and "me" repeatedly.
Then again, there's the "Good Neighbor" prayer
Which allows you to get something accomplished
As a third party, entirely because you're a "Good Person."
And finally there's the prayer in which
You really have nothing to say,
But you know prayer is one of the Rules,
So you close your eyes, think of God,
And drift off to sleep without a word.
They're all available to you free of charge,
And if they don't work, let us hear from you.
We're in the Yellow Pages under "W":
WE'VE THOUGHT FOR OVER 2000 YEARS
THAT WE HAD GOD PAINTED INTO A VERY SMALL CORNER.

IMITATION: ELIZABETHAN SONNET

I love you most the times I think of death,
Of leaving you or having you leave me.
And though I hope to breathe a holy breath
In what Tradition calls Eternity,
Real is the separation we await.
It is romanticized: a flower-strewn grave,
Teary-eyed dreamings at a garden gate.
They come to soothe but do not come to save.
That anguished parting I will hold in mind,
And try to weave into my plan of life,
For waking on some morning I may find
That I have lost my lover and my wife.
Such preparation will my way attend,
Till all Time's seeming endings have their end.

ST. JULIAN OF NORWICH

"All shall be well!" St. Julian cried.
All shall be well, indeed.
It was the Christ who told her so,
And this became a Creed.

For all is all, it surely is,
And not to be denied,
That Gates of Hell cannot hold back
This beatific tide.

Yet head and heart can never join
When saints do not say well,
That most who ever walked the earth
Now writhe in Jesus' Hell.

Julian of Norwich (1342–1416), English anchorite, wrote *Revelations of Divine Love*

I LEARN LIFE

I learn life is indifferent
To if I live or die.
And I can hold my head erect,
Or hang my head and sigh.

But if I choose to stand and straight,
Or if I choose lament,
I am assured a loving God
Is not indifferent.

I do not doubt it; ages roll,
And sorrows rise and fall.
But, oh, one stops my breaking heart,
And nothing helps at all.

SEXUAL ASSAULT

We taught you this: be beautiful and sexy,
But charming and "good."
False dichotomies, and now you know.
Yet, none of us knew how to shuffle them together,
Exactly where they merged.
Regardless, it cannot come to this:
You should not be hurt, Ever!
You see what a complex of problems it is.
You see our dilemma and profound failure.
Surely, you see our impotent guilt.
You must understand it, Child,
For dutifully we are here with you,
In sackcloth and ashes,
Wringing our pious, spiritual hands
As you lie weeping in the tragic bed,
Scratched and bruised and crying,
"Unclean! Unclean!"

REFLECTIONS ON MERLEAU-PONTY

I read Maurice Merleau-Ponty
And his phenomenology
Of how our bodies situate
And one to another relate;
How in the world we beings sit:
It comes to us, we go to it.
Our meaning thus we delegate,
And we our own worlds do "create":
How language is a gift to us,
We use definitional trust.
Unlike Descartes, we cannot flout
All things; in fact, we cannot doubt
That others are, some things exist,
For if we do then we have missed
The fact that we are creatures bound
By our own existential ground.
"I think, therefore I am," a cry
Of one unordained spirit's eye
Who split the world in one fell stroke
While speaking what no "body" spoke.

Maurice Merleau-Ponty (1908–1961), French philosopher, wrote
The Primacy of Perception

ON A KLIMT

I close my eyes
I fix my lips
I place my hands
Upon your hips
I pull you close
I drink you in
In one long draught
In sip
Sip
Sips

Gustav Klimt (1862–1918), Austrian artist, painted "The Kiss"

SWEETNESS OF THE NIGHT

The sweetness of the night
Is never lost to day,
And turning Earth assures
Its sweet return alway.

But I have often read
Of lands without a night,
But that cannot be bliss
Regardless of the light.

So if the blue Earth burns
And stars fall in the sea,
There must be darkness still
For lovers and for me.

THE SPIRIT AND THE FLESH

"The Spirit strong, the Flesh is weak":
I think it written wrong.
The Spirit is a timid thing,
But, oh, the Flesh is strong.

So when the saints drone on and on,
Believe not what you heard.
Yet, it was not so long ago
That Flesh became the Word.

FREEZING

Pure Winter white is the absence of color,
Save the clumps of tenacious green
Spread like moss on the Arctic field.
(That your breast could succor my sorrows.)
And in the distance towns arise,
In the distance cities spring.
In their images pure snow is absence.
(That your heart could ease my yearnings.)
With the rampaging wind comes dust,
White dust which is absence of color,
Blowing through this space of Life,
The space of things and persons
Who taste this sweet, dry spray.
(Oh, that your hands could hold my heartaches.)
Through shoes of wood these absences crush,
Solid, formidable as any foe.
Through gloves of skin these spaces freeze
And stiffen failing fingers.
(That your lips could kill my evils;
That your love could flow like wine!)
Pure white is the absence,
White is the color of colors,
And I am the animal of this space
Whose blood slows through the pure of. . ..
(That your warm blood could flow through veins.)

Pure is the color of colors.
Slow is this death of freezing.
Death is the absence of living.
How my life grows sleepy in the distant room.
(Oh, that soft arms could hold me at your dying.)

ONLY SON

There is a grave some miles away
Where I have laid a son.
And Summers on hot afternoons
I'd walk the stones among.

He has a lamb beside his name,
And I suppose the theme
Is that a gentle Shepherd now
Holds him—or one can dream.

"The child is father to the man":
I never understood,
Until I laid him tenderly
And prayed for timeless good.

I now believe, eternally,
That children all grow up,
And chaperone us ages on
To drain the dreg-filled cup.

Quotation from work by William Wordsworth (1770—1850),
English poet

THE RICH YOUNG RULER

"Sell everything you own," he said,
"Then come and follow me."
The troubled rich young ruler spoke:
"I am not quite that free."

The Master touched him on the arm,
"We can negotiate!
No talk of shiny needle eyes,
Nor camels at the gate."

In truth, it happened otherwise,
And stings me to this day,
That Jesus loved him sore enough
To let him walk away.

Story in Synoptic Gospels

PONTIUS PILATE

I saw a tree that hungered for a man.
I saw a man who hungered for a cause.
I saw a king who used such sleight of hand,
They crucified him under his own laws.

Roman Procurator when Jesus was crucified

CRUCIFIXION

"I will see to it you are never taken and put to death."
"Get Thee behind me, Satan!"
"Yes, Lord, yes."

His is a handsome, kingly head.
The crown is spiny, odd.
Laugh, crowd, for he is guilty.
Yell, shout, spit, curse.
What goes before you is evil!
Let him try it on.

For the thorns are sharp
And the blood is free
And the blood runs red
For you and me

Throw down that cross!
It is your vehicle,
Your "Holy Seat."
The large hands and feet are dirty, not clean.
Strong hands are beautiful in the sunlight.
They will do.
Place the nails at the wrist
And strike, Hammer, strike.
Yes!
Straighten his legs.

The nail on the foot:
Your laughing JOB, Centurion.
Strike again to be sure
That this Jesus is secure.

For the nails are sharp
And the blood is free
And the blood runs red
For you and me

Push up, criminal Jesus,
On the nails in your feet.
Your chest cavity has sagged
And to breathe you must PUSH.
Ha! Your strength is going fast.

So now, breathing your last,
Hear this our Benediction:
We declare you a derelict, blasphemer, sinner.
You are cut off from God to the
Outer pangs of Hell forever.
Anathema!!!

Walk faster, Roman free man.
Push the spear—yes.
It is shiny and smooth.
No movement, nothing.
Nothing at all.
He is, wretched one, forever dead!

It is finished.
For the spear is sharp
And the blood is free
And the blood runs red
For you and me

Epilogue

Three days later, the whale expelled,
And the Incarnate God Almighty
Stretched out his arms:
"See the scars in my feet and hands:
I created all the little fishes."

Amen and Amen.

www.ingramcontent.com/pod-product-compliance
Lightning Source LLC
Chambersburg PA
CBHW071736040426
42446CB00012B/2380